LOW VOICE

12 SACRED VOCAL SOLOS
FOR CLASSICAL SINGERS

ISBN 978-1-4584-1381-9

G. SCHIRMER, *Inc.*

DISTRIBUTED BY

HAL•LEONARD®
CORPORATION

7777 W. BLUEMOUND RD. P.O. BOX 13819 MILWAUKEE, WI 53213

www.schirmer.com
www.halleonard.com

CONTENTS

Pianist on the CD:
Laura Ward

AIN'T GOT TIME TO DIE

Words and Music by
Hall Johnson
piano accompaniment by John Purifoy

Adapted as a solo for this edition.

4

when I'm heal-in' de sick,_____ when I'm

heal-in' de sick,_ I'm prais - in' my Je - sus, Ain' got time to die. 'Cause_ it takes

all o' ma time_ to praise my Je - sus, all o' ma time_ to praise my Lord. If

I don' praise_ Him de rocks gon-ter cry out, "Glo-ry an' hon - or,

*Sing: Glorian hon-nuh!

givin' my all, __ I'm serv - in' my Mas - ter, Ain' got time to

die. 'Cause __ it takes all o' ma time __ to praise my Je - sus,

all o' ma time __ to praise my Lord. If I don' praise __ Him de

rocks gon - ter cry out, "Glo - ry an' hon - or, glo - ry an' hon - or!"

Ain' got time to die. Now, won't you git out o' ma way,— lem-me praise ma Je-sus? Out o' ma way!— Let-me praise my Lord. If I don' praise Him de rocks gon-ter cry out, "Glo-ry an' hon-or, glo-ry an' hon-or!" Ain' got time to die!

AVE MARIA

Franz Schubert

BE THOU MY VISION

Ancient Irish
translated by Mary E. Byrne, 1905
versified by Eleanor H. Hull, 1912

Traditional Irish Melody
arranged by Joel K. Boyd

Wak - ing or sleep - ing, thy __ pres - ence, my light. ____

Be thou my __ wis - dom, and thou my true word;

I ev - er with thee and thou with me, Lord:

Thy my__ great Fa - ther, and I thy true son;__

Thou in me dwell - ing and__ I with thee one.__

Rich - es I__ heed not, or man's emp - ty praise, Thou mine in -

victo - ry won, May I reach heav - en's joys, O bright heav'n's

sun! Heart of ___ my ___ own heart, what - ev - er be -

fall, _____ Still be my vi - sion, O ___ ru - ler of

all. _____

COME SUNDAY

Spiritual from *Black, Brown and Beige*

Duke Ellington
adapted by Lawrence Rosen

a tempo

Lord, Dear Lord a - bove: God Al - might - y, God of Love.

p

Ped.   ✻ Ped. sim.

ossia
8va -

Please look down and see my peo - ple through. _____

poco

più poco animato

1. I be - lieve that God put sun and moon up in the
2. Heav - en is a good - ness time, a bright - er light on

poco ***mf***

* Alternate rhythm: ♩ ♩ ♩. ♪

sky.
I don't mind the gray skies 'Cause they're
high.
(Spoken)Do unto others as you would have them do to you:
(Sing) And

1. *poco rit.*
just clouds pass - ing by.
have a bright - er

2. *poco rit.*
by and by.

a tempo
Lord, Dear Lord a - bove: God Al - might - y, God of Love,

Please look down and see my peo-ple through. _____

più poco animato

I be-lieve God is now, was then and al-ways will be.

With God's bless-ing we can make it through e-ter-ni-

Alternate rhythm: ♩ ♩ ♩ ♪

ty. Lord, Dear Lord a - bove: God Al - might - y, God of

Love, Please look down and see my peo - ple through.

*Alternate rhythm: ♩ ♩ ♩. ♪

CREATE IN ME A CLEAN HEART, O GOD

Psalm 51: 10-13

Carl Mueller

and re - new a right spir - it with - in me.

Cast me not a - way from Thy pres - ence; and take not Thy ho - ly spir - it from me.

Poco animato

Re - store un - to me the joy of Thy sal -
va - tion, re - store _____ the joy, _____
re - store un - to me the joy of Thy sal -
va - tion; and up - hold _____ me, up - hold _____

me with Thy free _____ spir - it, Thy free _____

spir - it. Then will I teach trans - gres - sors Thy

Moderato

ways; and sin - ners shall be con - vert - ed un - to

Più lento

Thee. Cre - ate in me a clean heart, O God!

"Overlook Acre"
Little Silver, N.J.
July, 1956

MY LORD, WHAT A MORNIN'

African-American Spiritual
arranged by Hall Johnson

With mystic expectation

The musical form of this edition has been slightly adapted from Johnson's original.

Verses

fall. *f* 1.You'll hear de trum - pet soun' To wake de
mf 2.You'll hear de sin - ners moan To see de

na - tions un - der - groun', Look - in' to my God's right
right - eous march - in' home,

han' When de stars be - gin to fall.

Coda

fall.

PANIS ANGELICUS

César Frank

gratefully dedicated to my friend John Charles Thomas

THE LORD'S PRAYER

Albert Hay Malotte

PRAISE THE LORD! YE HEAVENS, ADORE HIM

Anonymous

Hyfrydol
Rowland Prichard
arranged by Joshua Parman

PRAYER OF THE NORWEGIAN CHILD

Olaf Trojörgson

Richard Kountz

THERE IS A BALM IN GILEAD

African-American Spiritual
arranged by Hall Johnson

Calm and a bit free

The musical form of this edition has been slightly adapted from Johnson's original.

soul. 1. Some - times I feel dis - cour - aged And

think my work's in vain, But then the Ho - ly

Refrain

Spir - it re - vives my soul a - gain. ____ There is a

balm in Gil - e - ad To make the wound - ed

whole. ___ There ___ is a balm in Gil - e - ad To

heal the sin - sick soul. 2. If you can't preach like

Pe - ter, If you can't pray like Paul, Go

home an' tell your neigh - bor He died to save us

THE 23RD PSALM

Albert Hay Malotte

his name's sake.

Adagio (mournfully)

Yea, tho' I walk thro' the val - ley of the shad - ow of

heavily

poco accel.

Suddenly much faster (with conviction)

death, I will fear no e - vil: for

f sostenuto

Più mosso

o - ver. Sure - ly

Allegro moderato (joyously)

good - ness and mer - cy shall fol - low me

all _____ the days of my life: _____ and I will

Moderato (with exalted confidence)   **Very slowly and with great feeling**

dwell _____ in the house of the Lord for

Still very slowly

ev - er, and ev - er -

Tempo I° ($\quad$ = 72)

more. _____

About the Enhanced CD

In addition to piano accompaniments playable on both your CD player and computer, this enhanced CD also includes tempo and pitch adjustment software for computer use only. This software, known as the Amazing Slow Downer, was originally created for use in pop music to allow singers and players the freedom to independently adjust both tempo and pitch elements. Because we believe there may be valuable educational use for these features in classical and theatre music, we have included this software as a tool for both the teacher and student. For quick and easy installation instructions of this software please see below.

In recording a piano accompaniment we necessarily must choose one tempo. Our choice of tempo, phrasing, ritardandos, and dynamics is carefully considered. But by the nature of recording, it is only one choice. Similar to our choice of tempo, much thought and research has gone into our choice of key for each song.

However, we encourage you to explore your own interpretive ideas, which may differ from our recordings. This new software feature allows you to adjust the tempo up and down without affecting the pitch. Likewise, the Amazing Slow Downer allows you to shift pitch up and down without affecting the tempo. We recommend that these new tempo and pitch adjustment features be used with care and insight. Ideally, you will be using these recorded accompaniments and the Amazing Slow Downer for practice only.

The audio quality may be somewhat compromised when played through the Amazing Slow Downer. This compromise in quality will not be a factor in playing the CD audio track on a normal CD player or through another audio computer program.

INSTALLATION FROM DOWNLOAD:

For Windows (XP, Vista or 7):
1. Download and save the .zip file to your hard drive.
2. Extract the .zip file.
3. Open the "ASD Lite" folder.
4. Double-click "setup.exe" to run the installer and follow the on-screen instructions.

For Macintosh (OSX 10.4 and up):
1. Download and save the .dmg file to your hard drive.
2. Double-click the .dmg file to mount the "ASD Lite" volume.
3. Double-click the "ASD Lite" volume to see its contents.
4. Drag the "ASD Lite" application into the Application folder.

INSTALLATION FROM CD:

For Windows (XP, Vista or 7):
1. Load the CD-ROM into your CD-ROM drive.
2. Open your CD-ROM drive. You should see a folder named "Amazing Slow Downer." If you only see a list of tracks, you are looking at the audio portion of the disk and most likely do not have a multi-session capable CD-ROM.
3. Open the "Amazing Slow Downer" folder.
4. Double-click "setup.exe" to install the software from the CD-ROM to your hard disk. Follow the on-screen instructions to complete installation.
5. Go to "Start," "Programs" and find the "Amazing Slow Downer Lite" application. Note: To guarantee access to the CD-ROM drive, the user should be logged in as the "Administrator."

For Macintosh (OSX 10.4 or higher):
1. Load the CD-ROM into your CD-ROM drive.
2. Double-click on the data portion of the CD-ROM (which will have the Hal Leonard icon in red and be named as the book).
3. Open the "Amazing OS X" folder.
4. Double-click the "ASD Lite" application icon to run the software from the CD-ROM, or copy this file to your hard drive and run it from there.

MINIMUM SOFTWARE REQUIREMENTS:

For Windows (XP, Vista or 7):
Pentium Processor: Windows XP, Vista, or 7; 8 MB Application RAM; 8x Multi-Session CD-ROM drive

For Macintosh (OS X 10.4 or higher):
Power Macintosh or Intel Processor; Mac OS X 10.4 or higher; MB Application RAM; 8x Multi-Session CD-ROM drive